First published in the UK in 1999 by
Belitha Press Limited, London House,
Great Eastern Wharf, Parkgate Road,
London SW11 4NQ

ISBN 1 84138 027 X

British Library Cataloguing in Publication Data for
this book is available from the British Library.

Printed in China

Editor: Veronica Ross
Designer: Rosamund Saunders
Picture Researcher: Diana Morris
Consultant: Sallie Purkis
Illustrator: Jackie Harland

PHOTO CREDITS
AAA Collection: 11c, 11b, 23b, 24b. AKG London: 4br, 22tl, 22cr,
29t. Ashmolean Museum, Oxford/ Bridgeman Art Library: back
cover, 5br, 7bl. Tom Bean/Tony Stone Images: 29b. Gérard
Blot/RMN: 2, 17. British Museum/Bridgeman Art Library:
29cr/Werner Forman Archive: 27b. Bob Campbell/Tony Stone
Images: 5bl. Donald Cooper/Photostage: 14. Corbis: front cover
tr, 6cr, 13t, 13b. C.M. Dixon: 6br, 8bl, 9tl, 10cl,19bl. Mary Evans
PL: 23c. Galleria dell Accademia, Firenze/Erich Lessing/AKG
London: 26cl. Gamma/ J.O/FSP: 12t. George Grigoriou/Tony
Stone Images: front cover b, 27c. David Hanson/Tony Stone
Images: 4bl. House of Commons Education Unit: 10b, Parl. ©
1995. Hulton Getty Archive: 21t. Hutchison Library: 22. Leeds
Museums & Galleries/Bridgeman Art Library: 28. Dr Erwin
Mueller/SPL: 21br. Musée des Beaux Arts, Grenoble/Bridgeman
Art Library:18l. Musée Vivenal, Compiegne/AKG London/Erich
Lessing: 3bl, 12b. Museo Archeologico Nazionale, Napoli/ AKG
London: 8br. Museo Archeologico Nazionale, Napoli/ Roger-
Viollet/Bridgeman Art Library: 7t, 15t,18br. Museo della Civilta
Romana, Roma/Roger-Viollet/Bridgeman Art Library: 16bl.
Museo Nazionale Romano delle Terme/AKG London: 6cl, 9br.
David Nunuk/SPL: 20cr. Powerstock/Zefa:1, 6bl, 7br,1 5bl, 15cr,
16cr. Chris Priest/SPL: 24t. Gary Prior/Allsport: 3br. Andy
Sacks/Tony Stone Images: 19cr. Sporting Pictures: front bl.
Vatican Museums & Galleries/Bridgeman Art Library: 20bl.
Randy Well/Tony Stone Images: front cover t, 26b.

THE DATES IN THIS BOOK
BC (Before Christ) is used with dates of events that
happened before the birth of Christ. AD (Anno Domini,
from the Latin for 'in the year of our Lord') is used with
dates of events that happened after the birth of Christ.
The letter c used in the text stands for the Latin word
circa, and means about.

Some of the more unfamiliar words used in this book
are explained in the glossary on page 30.

CONTENTS

Introduction

A legacy is something handed down from one person or generation to another. It may be an object, a lifestyle or a way of thinking. The Ancient Greeks lived thousands of years ago, but the legacy of their brilliant culture still lives on today. We study their works of history and philosophy. Their ideas on maths and science still influence modern technology. Many great buildings are built in Greek style. And many modern governments are democracies, a system of politics first used in Ancient Greece.

FAMOUS PEOPLE

The first major Greek civilization grew up on the island of Crete. It was called Minoan, after Minos, its legendary king. It was rediscovered by a British archaeologist, Sir Arthur Evans, in the late nineteenth century. His excavations at the magnificent royal palace at Knossos showed us, for the first time, how the Minoans lived.

Sir Arthur Evans at work.

◄ *The sprawling modern city of Athens. Many ruined buildings still remain from Athens' ancient past. They have provided us with vital clues about how the Greeks lived.*

Who were the Greeks?

The Ancient Greeks were the people who lived in Greece from about 2000 to 30 BC. Ancient Greece was not a united country. By the 700s BC, it had been divided into small city-states, each with its own rulers, army and coins. The cities fought each other for land and trade. But all Greeks spoke the same language, though there were many different dialects. They called themselves Hellenes and their country Hellas.

An island kingdom

Greece is made up of the mainland and hundreds of islands in the Aegean and Ionian seas. In ancient times, Greece also included parts of western Turkey and southern Italy. Overcrowding and lack of good farmland led many people to leave Greece and establish colonies overseas.

▼ *This map shows Ancient Greece and its position in the Mediterranean world.*

IMPACT

The historic ruins of Ancient Greece still have a very strong impact today. Every year, millions of tourists travel to Greece to visit the famous ancient sites, such as this temple dedicated to the goddess Athene, on the beautiful island of Rhodes.

The temple of Athene.

How do we know?

We know a great deal about the Ancient Greeks because they left so much behind. Archaeologists have excavated many Greek cities and found a huge range of objects, including thousands of pots, decorated with scenes from Greek mythology and everyday life.

▶ *An ancient Greek pot showing a shoemaker cutting leather for a shoe.*

5

KEY DATES IN

3000 BC | **2000 BC** | **1000 BC** | **800 BC**

c 2900-1000 BC The Bronze Age in Crete and Greece. People discover how to make bronze by mixing copper and tin. They use it to make tools and weapons.

c 2000 BC Minoan civilization flourishes on Crete and the first Minoan palaces are built. They are destroyed by earthquakes but later rebuilt.

c 1600 BC The Mycenaeans are at the height of their power on mainland Greece.

c 1450 BC Crete is invaded and conquered by the Mycenaeans.

c 1400 BC A huge volcanic eruption destroys all the Minoan palaces on Crete.

c 1250 BC The traditional date for the Trojan War.

c 1100 BC Decline of Mycenaean culture. The start of the Dark Ages in Greece. During this time the art of writing is lost, so there are no written records of this period.

c 800 BC The Archaic Period begins. Greek culture revives and starts to flourish. Writing is used again.

700s BC Greece is divided into many independent *polis*, or city-states. The most powerful are Athens and Sparta.

776 BC The first Olympic Games are held at Olympia in honour of the god Zeus.

c 700 BC The poet Homer composes *The Iliad* and *The Odyssey*. These are the earliest examples of Greek literature to survive.

ANCIENT GREECE

| 600 BC | 400 BC | 200 BC | 100 BC |

c 508 BC Democracy is introduced in Athens.

371 BC Sparta is defeated by Thebes which becomes the leading power in Greece.

c 500-336 BC The Classical Period. Greek culture reaches its height.

490-449 BC The Persian Wars. The Greeks are victorious. They defeat the Persians at the Battle of Marathon (490 BC) and the Battle of Salamis (480 BC).

362 BC Athens and Sparta join forces to defeat the Thebans.

338 BC At the Battle of Chaeronea, the Greek city-states are defeated by the Macedonians. Philip II of Macedonia unites Greece under his control and declares war against the Persians.

147-146 BC The Achaean War. The Romans conquer Greece.

479-431 BC The Golden Age of Athens. The city is rebuilt and grows rich from trade.

336 BC Philip is assassinated. His son, Alexander, succeeds him and builds a vast empire stretching from Greece to India in the east.

431-404 BC The Peloponnesian Wars between great rivals, Athens and Sparta. The Spartans win.

323 BC Alexander dies of a fever in Babylon.

c 323-30 BC The Hellenistic Period. Alexander's generals divide his empire between them.

THE STORY OF GREECE

The first great Greek civilization began on Crete in about 2000 BC. The Minoans had a highly organized society. They traded far and wide and grew very wealthy. Their towns were built around splendid palaces. The largest palace was built at a place called Knossos. By about 1450 BC many of the palaces had been destroyed and the Minoan civilization came to an end. We don't know why, but invading Mycenaeans may have brought about its destruction.

▲ The ruins of the ancient Minoan Palace of Knossos on the island of Crete, as it looks today.

FAMOUS PEOPLE

Alexander the Great became King of Macedonia, in north-east Greece, in 336 BC. He was a brilliant soldier and leader. In 13 years, he conquered a vast empire which stretched from Greece right across to India. Alexander died young in 323 BC, but his conquests helped to spread Greek culture further than ever before.

A Roman mosaic of Alexander the Great from Pompeii, Italy.

The Mycenaeans

The Mycenaeans dominated Greece from about 1600-1100 BC. They built huge hill-top cities, protected by thick stone walls. They are named after the greatest of these, Mycenae. In about 1200 BC, Mycenaean society was destroyed by famine and civil wars. Greece entered a time of decline called the Dark Ages which lasted until about 800 BC. This was followed by the Archaic Period (c 800-500 BC) which brought new prosperity.

◄ The Lion Gate at Mycenae, the main gateway to the walled city.

IMPACT

We use the word labyrinth to mean a maze. But it actually comes from a Greek word for axe. Axes were used to decorate Minoan palaces which may have seemed like mazes because they had so many winding corridors. According to legend, the labyrinth at Knossos was home to the terrible minotaur: half man, half bull.

Classical Greece

The Classical Period (c 500-336 BC) was a golden age for Greece. Greek culture flourished and, in the Persian Wars, the Greeks defeated the Persians, their arch enemies. This is the part of Greek history we know most about from art, sculpture and writing.

The Hellenistic Period

The Hellenistic Period (c 323-30 BC) followed the death of Alexander the Great. His generals split his vast empire between them. By 146 BC, the Romans had conquered Greece. The Romans greatly admired Greek culture. They copied many Greek sculptures and manuscripts, keeping Greek ideas alive even when the originals were lost.

◄ A Roman copy of a statue of the goddess Juno, originally made by the Greek sculptor, Praxiteles.

HAVING A SAY

Each year ten *strategoi*, or military commanders, were elected to put new laws into action. The most famous was Pericles (c 495-429 BC). A brilliant general and politician, he was elected to office every year from 443-429 BC. He was such a powerful speaker, he was almost always able to win the public over to his way of thinking.

A bust of Pericles, one of the most popular leaders of Ancient Athens.

The governments of many modern countries, such as Britain and the USA, are called democracies. This means that people can choose who they want to govern their country. The name democracy comes from two Greek words, *demos*, or people, and *kratos*, or rule. This ancient form of government was first used in Athens in 508 BC.

▼ *Inside the Houses of Parliament in London. The British system of government is an example of a modern democracy.*

How democracy worked

In a modern democracy, everybody has a say. But in Athens, only male citizens could vote. Women, foreigners and slaves were excluded. New laws and policies were drawn up by the 500 elected members of the Council. These were then debated in the Assembly, which met every ten days. At least 6000 citizens had to be present for a meeting to begin. If numbers were low, people were dragged in off the streets!

IMPACT

In a modern multi-party democracy, voters choose between candidates from several different parties to represent them in government. In a presidential republic, such as the USA, people also vote for the head of state, or president. India is the largest democracy in the world with about 600 million people able to vote.

Greek society

In Athens, society was divided into groups – citizens, metics and slaves. Citizens, men with Athenian parents, had the most rights and could vote and speak in the law courts. Metics were men born outside the city. They had no say in the government. Most slaves were prisoners of war. They had no rights at all. Women were treated as non-citizens, with no right to express opinions of their own.

Ostracism

To remove corrupt or unpopular politicians, the Greeks used a system called ostracism. Each year citizens in the Assembly wrote the names of bad politicians on broken pieces of pottery called *ostraka*. If more than 6000 votes were cast against someone, he was banished for ten years. We still use the word ostracize to mean to leave out or exclude someone.

▲ An ostrakon (the singular of ostraka) showing the name of a politician called Aristeides.

▲ The ruins of the Tholos in Athens, the building where the Council met to draw up new laws and policies.

GOING FOR GOLD

Every four years the world's greatest athletes compete in the Olympic Games. After months of training, this is their chance to win Olympic gold and glory. They are following an ancient tradition. The first ever Olympic Games were held at Olympia, in Greece, in 776 BC, in honour of the god Zeus.

Training begins

The games lasted for five days in summer. Athletes and trainers from all over Greece travelled to Olympia to take part, together with thousands of spectators. Women were not allowed to compete, or even to watch the games. If they were caught doing so, they were thrown off a cliff as punishment. A truce was called between rival Greek city-states so that athletes could attend the games safely.

▲ The USA's Michael Johnson, gold medal winner in the 200 and 400 metres at the 1996 Atlanta Olympics. Johnson is one of the greatest modern Olympians.

◄ A vase painting showing athletes competing in a race at the ancient Olympics. Running was the oldest event in the games.

FAMOUS PEOPLE

The modern Olympic marathon is run over a distance of 42.19 kilometres. It was not included in the ancient games. The first ever marathon runner was an Athenian soldier called Pheidippides. In 490 BC, he ran 40 kilometres, non-stop, from Marathon to Athens with the news that the Greeks had beaten the Persians in battle.

▲ *The running track at Olympia as it looks today. In ancient times, 40,000 spectators could watch the action from banks of seats around the track.*

The main events

The main events in the ancient Olympics were running, wrestling, horse and chariot racing, boxing and the pentathlon. The pentathlon consisted of five events – running, wrestling, long jump, javelin and discus. The star event was the sprint. Athletes ran one length of the track, a distance of 192 metres. The most dangerous event was the pankration, a mixture of boxing and wrestling. Any tactic was allowed, apart from eye-gouging and biting.

Winners and prizes

Prizes were awarded on the last day of the games. Ancient Olympic champions were not given medals. Instead, they received an olive crown, cut from the sacred tree, and had a statue displayed in their honour at Olympia. Many became professional athletes, sponsored by their home cities. They were very well paid for their efforts.

◄ *This statue shows a discus thrower. The discus was one of five events in the pentathlon. At today's games it is one of ten events in the decathlon.*

CURTAIN UP

The word theatre comes from the Greek word *theatron*, meaning a place for seeing. The story of theatre as we know it today begins more than 2000 years ago in Ancient Greece. Songs and dances were performed as part of a religious festival, held in honour of the god Dionysus. Gradually, these developed into plays.

FAMOUS PEOPLE

The top Greek writer of comedies was Aristophanes (c 445-388 BC). He used ordinary people as characters who poked fun at politicians and intellectuals. In many of Aristophanes' plays, the chorus was composed of actors dressed as animals, such as frogs or birds. The word comedy comes from the Greek word *komoidia* which means merry-making.

▼ *Actors in a modern production of the Oresteia, a group of three plays by the ancient Greek playwright Aeschylus (c 525-455 BC).*

Plays and playwrights

From the middle of the sixth century BC, the festival included a drama competition. Plays were entered in two categories – tragedy and comedy. Both were extremely popular. The works of the great Greek playwrights, such as Aristophanes (comedy), and Sophocles, Euripides and Aeschylus (tragedy), are still performed today.

◀ *Sophocles (c 496-406 BC) was one of the greatest playwrights of Ancient Greece. He wrote more than 100 tragedies.*

An actor's life

Only men were allowed to become actors. They played every role, including those of women. Some actors played leading roles. Others were part of a group called the chorus. They sang, danced and commented on the action. Actors wore masks to show the type of character they were playing. To change from a happy character to a sad one, an actor changed his mask. The theatres were very large and the actors often padded their costumes and wore large wigs to make themselves more visible.

IMPACT

Many modern theatres and concert halls are based on the horseshoe shape of ancient Greek theatres. This shape offers all the spectators a good view of the stage, and also gives excellent acoustics. Some Greek theatres, such as the ancient Greek theatre at Epidaurus, have now been restored and are once again being used for drama festivals.

The Royal Theatre in Copenhagen, Denmark, uses the horseshoe shape of an ancient Greek theatre.

Taking your seat

Huge, open-air theatres were built all over Greece. Most could hold at least 18,000 spectators. The audience sat in a semi-circle around the stage. Stone tokens were used as tickets and were marked with a seat number. The best seats were in the front row. These were reserved for important officials and visitors, and for the competition judges.

◀ *The ancient theatre at Epidaurus, Greece, built on a hillside. Plays are still performed there today.*

15

READING AND WRITING

Many of the words we use today are borrowed from Ancient Greek. For example, cosmos is Greek for world; gymnasium is Greek for sports' training ground. Even the word alphabet comes from the Greek for the first two letters of the alphabet, alpha (Δ) and beta (ß).

FAMOUS PEOPLE

Two of the most famous works of Greek literature were composed by Homer, in the 700s BC. These were two long poems, *The Iliad* and *The Odyssey*. *The Iliad* tells the story of the Trojan War. *The Odyssey* tells of the travels of the hero, Odysseus, after the war. Both are still read today.

A copy of the wooden horse which won the Trojan War for the Greeks.

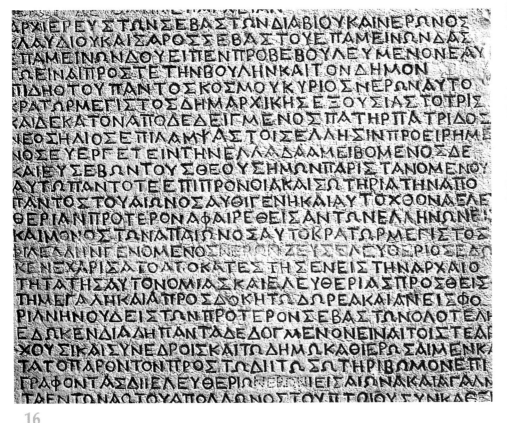

◄ A Greek translation of a speech given by the Roman emperor, Nero. The Romans wrote in Latin, basing their alphabet on that of the Greeks.

IMPACT

We still use Greek letters as mathematical symbols. The letter π (pi) is used to work out the circumference of a circle (the distance around the edge) from its radius (the distance from the middle to the edge). The equation used is: $c = 2\pi r$ ($2 \times \pi \times r$). Pi is usually given a value of 3.14. This was first calculated by another Ancient Greek, the mathematician, Archimedes (see page 22).

Speaking Greek

The Ancient Greeks all spoke the same language, although different regions had different dialects. When Greek was first written down, in the eighth century BC, it was mainly written in Attic, the dialect of Athens. The Greeks were very proud of their language. They called non-Greek speakers barbarians.

▶ *This statue shows a Greek scribe (writer) at work.*

Greek letters

The alphabet we use to write English is based on a Roman version of the Greek alphabet. In turn, the Greeks based their alphabet on that of the Phoenicians, who were traders from the Middle East. The Greeks had to add vowels – the Phoenicians only used consonants. At first, the Greeks wrote from right to left. Then they tried changing direction at the end of each line. From the sixth century BC, Greek was written from left to right.

Greek writers

Ancient Greek writers produced many works, from plays and poetry, to history and essays on politics and philosophy. They wrote on papyrus made from plants. This rotted easily so very few original manuscripts have survived. We know so much about Greek writing because, from Roman times onwards, people made copies of Greek works on vellum. Since then, these have been translated into hundreds of different languages.

Wisdom and Scholars

FAMOUS PEOPLE

The Greek author Herodotus was one of the first people to write a history book. In the fifth century BC, he wrote an account of the Persian Wars, between Persia and Greece, based on interviews with survivors.

He was also a great traveller, writing about his journeys to Egypt and beyond. His books about Egypt contained a detailed account of mummification.

The mummy of an Egyptian king. Bodies were mummified to preserve them for the next life.

Philosophy is the study of human nature and of the universe. It is concerned with thought, knowledge and reason. Philosophers try to answer difficult questions such as 'What is the meaning of life?' and 'How do we know things really exist?' The Ancient Greeks were the first philosophers, meaning lovers of knowledge. Their ideas and theories still affect our lives today.

▶ *A Roman mosaic showing the Greek philosopher, Plato, teaching at the Academy in Athens. Students came from far and wide to hear him speak.*

18

Finding a reason

The Greek philosophers were the first people to question the world around them and try to make sense of it using thought and logic. Before this, people explained life and nature in terms of the gods and their actions. The philosophers also looked at how people should try to live and behave, and how countries should be governed.

Famous thinkers

The most important Greek philosophers were Socrates, Plato and Aristotle. Their works are still widely read and studied. Socrates (c 469-399 BC) taught by asking his listeners questions about good and evil. But his ideas made him unpopular in Athens and he was forced to kill himself by drinking poison.

Brilliant students

Socrates never wrote down his ideas, but they were recorded by his pupils, who included Plato. In his most famous work, *The Republic*, Plato (c 429-347 BC) wrote about the ideal way of governing a city-state. Plato's most brilliant pupil was Aristotle (c 384-322 BC). Like Plato, he wrote about politics and society, but was also interested in poetry and science. He later became teacher to Alexander the Great.

IMPACT

Students came from far and wide to hear the philosophers speak. They usually taught in buildings called *gymnasia*. These started off as sports' training grounds, but later included lecture halls and libraries. In the fourth century BC, Plato and Aristotle set up two famous schools in Athens, called the Academy and the Lyceum. The first universities were based on these schools.

Graduation day at a modern university in the USA.

◄ *A head of Socrates, one of the greatest Greek philosophers. His ideas on truth, good and evil are still studied and debated today.*

SCIENCE AND MATHEMATICS

Some of the greatest scientists and mathematicians who have ever lived came from Ancient Greece. Many of their discoveries were so brilliant that they are still being used today. For example, many of the basic rules used in mathematics to calculate the sizes of triangles and circles were first worked out by the Ancient Greeks more than two thousand years ago.

FAMOUS PEOPLE

 In about 240 BC, the Greek astronomer Eratosthenes (c 276-194 BC), used geometry to calculate the circumference of the Earth at 40,250 kilometres. He was amazingly accurate. The Earth's actual circumference (through the Poles) is 40,007 kilometres.

Modern astronomers use sophisticated telescopes to study the sky and the stars.

◄ A painting by the Italian artist Raphael showing the great mathematician Pythagoras, surrounded by his students.

Pythagoras' triangles

The mathematician and philosopher, Pythagoras (c 580-500 BC), is still famous for the theorem (rule) on triangles which takes his name. This states that, in a right-angled triangle, the square of the hypotenuse (the longest side) equals the sum of the squares of the other two sides. This means that once you know the lengths of two sides of any right-angled triangle, you can work out the length of the third side.

◀ *Children are still taught Pythagoras' famous theorem, first devised 2500 years ago.*

Geometry genius

In about 300 BC, the mathematician Euclid (c 330-270 BC) wrote a famous book about geometry called *The Elements*. In it, he summed up the teachings of the mathematicians before him, including Pythagoras, and set out some of the most basic mathematical rules. *The Elements* was used by students as a text book for more than 2000 years.

Ancient astronomers

The Greeks were also outstanding astronomers. Long before anyone else, Anaxagoras (c 500-428 BC) realized that the Moon does not produce any light of its own but reflects the light of the Sun. Aristarchus (c 310-230 BC) worked out that the Earth spins on its axis and moves around the Sun. Nobody believed him at the time because he could not prove his theory.

IMPACT

As long ago as the 400s BC, the Greek physicist, Democritus (c 460-370 BC), claimed that everything was made of tiny fragments of matter called atoms. Democritus' theory was ignored for centuries until the modern study of atomic physics began in the early nineteenth century. It showed that Democritus had been right all along.

Atoms in a platinum crystal shown under a microscope.

AMAZING INVENTIONS

During the Hellenistic Period, a university called the Museum was built in the city of Alexandria, Egypt. It became the greatest centre of learning in the ancient world, with scholars coming from far and wide to work and study there. Scientists and engineers at the Museum invented many interesting devices. Some were impractical and quickly forgotten; others are still in use.

FAMOUS PEOPLE

One of the Museum's greatest scientists was Archimedes (see right). He invented a device, shaped like a large screw, which could raise water from one level to another. Water rose up through the screw as it was turned. Farmers in Egypt still use a device like this to irrigate their fields.

◀ This Egyptian farmer is using a modern version of the Archimedes' screw to draw water from the river for his fields.

Archimedes' screw

Archimedes (c 287-212 BC) was a skilled inventor, mathematician and astronomer. His most famous discovery was a law of physics, called the Archimedes Principle. This stated that an object displaces its own volume of water.

Archimedes is said to have discovered this while sitting in the bath and to have jumped out, shouting 'Eureka! Eureka!' ('I've got it! I've got it!').

▶ Archimedes in his famous bath.

Slot machines

Heron of Alexandria was called the machine man because of his vast number of inventions. Among them were mechanical toys and puppets, automatic sliding doors for temples, moving scenery for theatres, a water-powered organ and the world's first slot machine. It was designed for use in temples. In return for putting a coin in the slot, worshippers received some holy water for washing their hands and faces before they went inside.

Catapults and crossbows

Many of the Museum's inventors, including the great Philon of Byzantium, tried to produce better weapons. Among the most successful were catapults and crossbows. These shot stones and arrows further than the strongest human could throw, and were ideal for attacking cities or ships. Many later versions of these weapons were based on the ancient Greek designs.

IMPACT

The invention of the steam engine in the eighteenth century revolutionized transport and industry. But the first person to realize the usefulness of steam power was the Greek engineer, Heron of Alexandria, two thousand years before. His steam engine worked like this. Water was heated in a cauldron, producing steam which went up a pipe into a globe. The steam was forced out through another pipe, making the globe spin round at high speed.

Heron's famous steam machine built in the first century AD.

DOCTORS AND MEDICINE

FAMOUS PEOPLE

According to legend, Asclepius was the son of the Sun god, Apollo. He was brought up by a centaur (a creature with a horse's body and a man's head) who taught him about medicine. The goddess Athene gave Asclepius two phials of magic blood. One could kill anything. The other had the power to bring the dead back to life.

Asclepius, the ancient Greek god of medicine and healing.

Ancient Greek doctors were among the first to study illness and disease in a practical, scientific manner. Before this, people believed that diseases were sent by the gods as punishment, and that only the gods knew the cures. While respecting the gods, these early doctors pioneered a way of practising medicine which has lasted to the present day.

► *The temple of Asclepius on the island of Kos. Many Greeks visited the temple in hope that the god would cure them.*

Gods of healing

Most Ancient Greeks visited one of the temples of Asclepius, god of healing, if they were unwell. First, they washed and performed a sacrifice. Then they spent the night in the temple in the hope that Asclepius would appear in a dream and show them a cure. People who recovered left offerings. These were in the shape of a leg or ear, or whichever part of their body had been cured.

Hippocrates

The most famous Greek doctor was Hippocrates (c 460-377 BC). He lived on the island of Kos where he founded an important medical school. He taught his students to examine patients carefully and to find the scientific causes of their sickness. Then they prescribed a cure, often a herbal medicine, combined with advice about diet and exercise.

IMPACT

The code of ethics which doctors follow today is based on the Hippocratic Oath which Hippocrates made his students swear when they qualified as doctors. In it they promised to use medicine to heal people not harm them, not to give poison or carry out illegal operations, and not to betray a patient's confidence.

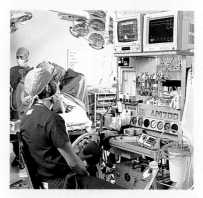

Inside a modern hospital.

Medicine at the Museum

Later Greek doctors working at the Museum (see page 22) also made many medical breakthroughs. In the third century BC, Herophilus and Erasistratus became the first to study how the human body works by dissecting actual bodies. (These belonged to criminals. They were often cut up alive!) Erasistratus also studied blood circulation. Their work was so advanced that it was not fully understood until centuries later.

► *A stone carving showing a selection of instruments from Ancient Greece. On either side are two cups, used to collect blood from patients.*

FAMOUS BUILDINGS

IMPACT

During the fifteenth to the seventeenth centuries, European architects, sculptors and artists such as Michelangelo, Leonardo da Vinci and Raphael, turned to Ancient Greece for inspiration. This period was called the Renaissance, which means rebirth, because it was as if Greek style and culture had been reborn.

Michelangelo's famous statue of David.

People who travel to Greece today can visit the ruins of many ancient Greek buildings, such as temples and theatres. Ordinary Greek houses were simple structures, and have not survived. But public buildings were very grand, and a great deal of money was spent on them. The building styles used by Greek architects can also be seen in many modern public buildings, such as parliament buildings and museums. These are called neo-classical buildings. Neo means new in ancient Greek. Classical means in Greek style.

► *The neo-classical US Capitol in Washington DC, USA.*

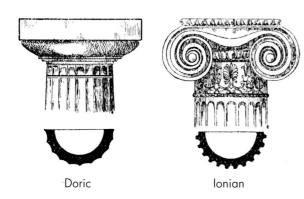

Doric   Ionian

Column styles

Stone columns were a vital part of Greek architecture. There were two main styles – Doric and Ionian. Doric columns were sturdy, with plain capitals (tops). Ionian columns were more elegant, and had capitals decorated with scroll-like carvings. The number of pillars, their height and spacing was carefully calculated for a balanced look.

The Acropolis

The Acropolis hill, topped by the Parthenon temple complex, still dominates the city of Athens as it did 2500 years ago. The Parthenon was built as a magnificent temple to Athene, the patron goddess of Athens. Building began in 447 BC and took ten years to complete. The temple is made of marble and was surrounded by a colonnade of 58 columns, many of which are still standing.

▲ *The ruins of the Parthenon today, standing on top of the Acropolis hill.*

Fabulous sculptures

All around the outside of the Parthenon ran a marble frieze, decorated with sculptures. These showed the procession of worshippers who, every four years, made their way to the temple as part of a great festival in Athene's honour. The background was originally painted, probably bright blue. You can see many of these sculptures in the British Museum in London.

▶ *Part of the marble frieze that ran around the Parthenon.*

FAMOUS PEOPLE

The frieze around the Parthenon was designed by the famous sculptor, Pheidias (c 500-425 BC). He also made the huge gold and ivory statue of Athene which stood inside. Pheidias was a close friend of Pericles (see page 10), who commissioned him to do the work. His brilliant career came to an end when he was accused of theft. He died in prison.

MYTHS AND LEGENDS

The Ancient Greeks knew and retold many stories about the lives and deeds of their gods, goddesses and heroes. These were called myths. Ever since then, Greek myths have been a great source of inspiration for artists, writers and musicians.

▼ *A painting called* The Return of Persephone *by the nineteenth-century artist Frederic Leighton.*

Demeter and Persephone

Demeter, goddess of crops and harvests, had a beautiful daughter, Persephone. When she was kidnapped by Pluto, god of the Underworld, Demeter was grief stricken. While she searched for Persephone, she let the crops die and people began to go hungry. The god Zeus persuaded Pluto to let Persephone return to Earth for six months of the year. These months are spring and summer. The other six, when Persephone returns to Pluto, are autumn and winter.

◄ *A painting by Franz von Stuck (1863-1928), showing Hercules killing the centaur Nessus.*

Twelve labours

The great hero Hercules was extremely strong and brave. To pay for killing his wife, he was set 12 impossible tasks, or labours. One of the labours was to kill a lion whose hide was so tough no weapon could pierce it. Hercules used his bare hands. When all the tasks were done, Hercules was free of his guilt.

Spiders and spinning

A princess, Arachne, boasted that she could weave better than the goddess, Athene. So Athene challenged her to a contest. Both wove their very best work. Furious that Arachne was indeed better than her, Athene tore her weaving up. Arachne was terrified and tried to kill herself. Filled with remorse, Athene saved Arachne and turned her into a spider. Now she could spin and weave to her heart's content. The group of animals to which spiders belong is called arachnids, after Arachne.

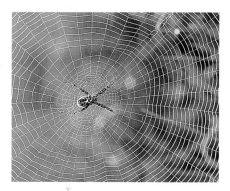

▲ *Named after an Ancient Greek princess, an arachnid (this is an orb weaver spider) shows off its spinning skills.*

GLOSSARY

acoustics How well sounds can be heard, for example in a theatre or concert hall. From the Greek word for to hear.

archaeologist A person who studies human history by excavating and examining ruins and remains, such as ancient cities, burial sites and artefacts, such as pots and tools.

Archaic Period The period in Ancient Greek history which lasted from about 800-500 BC.

Assembly A meeting of citizens in Athens at which they debated new laws and policies drawn up by an elected group of citizens called the Council.

astronomer A scientist who studies the stars, planets and other heavenly bodies.

atomic physics The scientific study of atoms, the tiny particles of matter which make up everything in the world.

axis An imaginary line which runs through the Earth from north to south, from the North Pole to the South Pole. The Earth spins round on its axis.

barbarians Any foreigners who did not speak Greek were called barbarians by the Greeks. The word came to be used for any uncivilized people.

cauldron A large, round metal pot used for cooking.

city-states Independent states which made up Ancient Greece. Each was made up of a city and the surrounding countryside, and had its own leaders and laws. The Greek word for city-state is *polis*.

civilization A society which is very advanced in science, technology, the arts, government and law.

civil wars Wars fought between two groups of people from the same city or country.

colonies Settlements established abroad by groups of Greeks when overcrowding and political problems forced them to leave their homes in Greece.

colonnade A row of columns along the front and sides of a building.

culture A country or people's achievements in the arts, sciences and technology.

Dark Ages The period in Ancient Greek history which lasted from about 1100-800 BC. It is called 'dark' because little is known about this time.

dialects Different forms or ways of speaking a language with their own pronunciation and sayings. Dialect is a Greek word which means conversation.

displace To move someone or something out of place, often by force.

empire A large and powerful state, often made up of several countries and territories. It is ruled over by a single leader called an emperor or empress.

ethics A set of rules which say how a person should behave in a particular situation. For doctors, ethics are the rules which tell them how they should treat their patients, for example by not betraying their confidence.

frieze A wide band of sculptures used to decorate a building, for example the famous frieze around the Parthenon in Athens.

geometry A branch of mathematics which studies the sizes and shapes of objects.

immortality Never dying but living forever. In Ancient Greece the gods were said to be immortal.

intellectuals Intelligent people with sharp, questioning minds.

irrigate To supply dry land with water. In dry countries, farmers have to irrigate their fields with water drawn from rivers, streams, or man-made channels, to make their crops grow.

logic The science of reasoning or working things out by careful thought and argument.

matter The substance which makes up everything in the universe.

mummification The Ancient Egyptian method of preserving dead bodies for the next world by embalming them with ointments and wrapping them in bandages.

myths Stories which are not based in historical fact but deal with supernatural characters, such as gods and heroes, their lives and their actions.

papyrus A type of reed which grows along the banks of the River Nile in Egypt and was used in ancient times to make paper.

patron Someone who gives money and support to another person, such as an artist or a writer, to help in their work.

phials Small glass bottles for medicine.

platinum A precious white metal.

reason A way of solving problems and drawing conclusions by using argument and debate.

republic A state or country that is ruled by elected leaders chosen by the people, rather than ruled by an unelected king.

right angle An angle of 90° made by two straight lines meeting, for example in a shape such as a square or triangle.

sacrifice The killing of an animal or person in honour of the gods.

society All the groups and classes of people living in a particular city or country.

truce An agreement to stop fighting or wars for a set period of time.

Underworld In Ancient Greek beliefs the Underworld was an underground kingdom where the souls of people went when they died. It was ruled over by the god Pluto.

vellum A fine sheet of material made from calf skin which was used for writing on in ancient times.

volume The amount of space an object takes up.

INDEX